Racing to Win

D0279418

Statistician

W. Foulsham & Co. Ltd.
London • New York • Toronto • Cape Town
Sydney

W. Foulsham & Company Limited
Yeovil Road, Slough, Berkshire, SL1 4JH

ISBN 0-572-01051-6

Printed in Great Britain by
St Edmundsbury Press Ltd, Bury St Edmunds

CONTENTS

SYSTEMS AND YOU

Racing is perhaps more popular now than ever
before. People of all kinds and classes follow the
Sport of Kings. Betting shops offer greater comfort
with improved facilities. They take their place in
every High Street and betting is now a respectable
pastime. Every big meeting receives extensive
television coverage. Small wonder that betting
turnover has reached record levels, even allowing for
inflation. In the year that I write nearly half a million
people gathered on Epsom Downs to watch the
Derby, the greatest race of them all. Whilst other
spectator sports experience grave difficulties, racing
has consolidated its position as our national sport.

So you like a bet. If you are honest, you will
admit that almost certainly you lose in the long run.
Most people do and the reason is simple. Unlike the
bookmaker who bets along methodical, businesslike
lines, the average punter stakes haphazardly
according to fancy. This is usually fatal and plays
right into the bookmaker's hands. If, on the other
hand, you are prepared to follow systems based on
established patterns of form and statistics, you give
yourself a chance of winning.

No system can pick a winner every time and even
the best methods are unlikely to yield more than a
marginal gain on outlay but that is still a lot better
than losing. Methodical betting along systematic
lines, although it cannot guarantee success, offers a
real prospect of a winning balance.

There are twelve systems outlined in this book.
Why twelve when one winning method will do? The
answer is of course that different styles of betting
appeal to different people. So you will find in these
pages systems for the Flat and systems for the

jumps. There are plans for favourites and plans for outsiders. Most focus on win only betting, whilst others cater for those who feel happier with each-way investments. A few go a stage further and are solely concerned with the staking as opposed to the selection aspect of backing horses. One attempts to exploit the excellent racing coverage to be found in the national press. In fact the twelve systems featured in the following pages cover the whole spectrum of racing. Whatever your betting preferences, you will find something here to interest you.

Each plan has full operating instructions and can be understood by anyone who has only a rudimentary knowledge of racing and betting. On the other hand the book as a whole, though easy to follow, is written very much from the expert point of view. Some experts scoff at systems. They point out that horses are not machines, that every system can be beaten sooner or later by the long losing run, that the bookmaker always wins in the end, and so on. Now it is certainly true that racing is notoriously unpredictable with the odds stacked against the punter and for these reasons no one should ever bet more than he can afford to lose on a system, however good it may appear.

Having said that, it is my belief that for the average punter who has no inside knowledge of the operations of a racing stable and no clue about secrets which are always jealously guarded, logical betting according to some plan based on racing know-how and horse sense is the only way to win. Most people follow racing for enjoyment but it is my experience that the pleasure is greatly increased when they manage to make a profit. If you have always lost in the past, then try a system. You will find it fun to operate and you may even be in the happy position of having the bookmaker pay for your pastime.

1
The 'SPECIALIST' System for winning bets on two-year-olds

Specialisation pays or so they say. Given the right temperament, this probably applies as much to betting matters as to any other sphere of activity. Certainly you could do a lot worse than to concentrate on one particular aspect of the racing scene for the majority of your bets. This is a great deal more sensible than jumping around from one expedient to another, clutching at every straw in the wind always in search of the elusive big win that so seldom materialises.

To my mind two-year-olds are an excellent medium for such an approach. Competing regularly over uniform sprint distances, juveniles run to form to a remarkable degree. They are fresh and bring to their racing a zest that is all too often lacking in older horses, many of which are definitely soured by over-exposure. By contrast consistency is the hallmark of two-year-old racing.

If you can be content with small but regular profits from fancied runners at the less spectacular end of the odds range, then it might well suit you to study the youngsters very closely. By going about it in the right way there is every chance that you could enjoy a successful season's betting with a sound capital gain at the end of the campaign to reward you for your efforts.

Two-year-olds perform within predictable limits to such an extent that a few simple tests can be used to pinpoint the best potential bets in a most effective way.

First, it is desirable that any two-year-old which carries your money should have won or been placed second on its previous run. Obviously in the course of a season's racing there are plenty of examples of youngsters which were third, fourth or unplaced last time out that go on to win their next race. On the other hand statistics show quite clearly that winners and seconds are quite outstanding. Here are the results of a survey for three full seasons:

LAST TIME OUT	PERCENTAGE OF WINS NEXT OUTING
first/second	43%
third/fourth	24%
unplaced	33%

When it is considered that firsts and seconds in the nature of things are vastly outnumbered by the others, then it is apparent that 43 is a very good percentage indeed. Clearly they offer a very high statistical chance of success.

Of course there are sound reasons for this excellent striking rate. Two-year-olds do reproduce their form more consistently than any other type of horse. If a youngster wins or finishes close up in a race, then unless it is asked to rise sharply in class there is every chance that it will be there or thereabouts in its next.

Over the same three-year period it was found that the win frequency for favourites in two-year-old non-handicaps (nursery handicaps were excluded because of their highly competitive nature) was 43.2% and for second favourites 24.1%. Note that both figures were adjusted to correct the discrepancy arising from the duplication which occurs when there are joint favourites or joint second favourites.

8

A combined percentage for winning first and second favourites of nearer seventy than sixty is so impressive that it seems pointless to look beyond it for the second rule of two-year-old betting. You are strongly advised to focus your attention only on the likely favourites, that is the first two in the betting forecast of a reliable sporting or daily paper.

A two-year-old, like any other thoroughbred, needs to be fully fit to do itself justice on the racecourse. However it is standard practice amongst all good trainers to give their charges a periodic rest. Horses are not machines; they cannot be kept at their racing best indefinitely without a break. In this respect they are no different to human beings who go to work regularly and need a holiday from time to time in order to recharge their batteries. The surest sign that a horse has been 'let down' is a prolonged period of absence from actual competition. When it does eventually return to racing after a lay-off it may have done a good deal of work at home but there is no substitute for a gallop under racing conditions to bring a horse right up to its absolute peak.

Therefore you are advised to back only two-year-olds which are running within one month of their previous public outing. This is a guarantee of a horse's racing fitness and enables you to be fairly certain that no complications have developed regarding general physical well-being which might detract from its ability to reproduce its form. The third rule goes a long way to ensuring that you are backing a horse which is fully fit and well.

The three conditions for betting in two-year-old non-handicaps may be summarised as follows:

1) Only back horses which finished first or second last out.

2) Concentrate on the first two in the betting forecast of the newspaper you use for racing purposes.

3) In no circumstances back any two-year-old which has not run in public for over a month (say 30 days).

These are rules from which you should not deviate. They will produce a short list of possibles from which to make your selection or selections each racing day. The final stage in the process is left to you. You may feel confident enough to rely on your personal reading of form and class. You may prefer to make use of the undoubted expertise of newspaper correspondents to arrive at your final choice. However there is one guide to which you would do well to pay particular attention. I refer to the comparative time test.

Two-year-old racing is peculiarly well suited to a close study of comparative times. Except for a few mile events late in the season, all juvenile races are decided over sprint distances and it is in sprints that time is of most value as an aid to finding winners. Riding tactics enter very little into calculations in races that are usually run flat out from start to finish. A two-year-old capable of recording a fast time should always be watched very closely.

Most readers will be familiar with the concept of comparative times by which each recorded race time can be classed as faster or slower than the standard for course and distance. The specialist racing press show this comparison in the following way:

Brighton   6f. I / 13.10s (a 3.10)
Goodwood   5f. I / 0.0s   (b 0.20)
Goodwood   6f. I / 15.10s (a 2.10)
Newmarket   7f. I / 27.94s (a 1.94)

The vital information is contained in the brackets. Here is shown the number of seconds and tenths of a second the winner was faster (b) or slower (a) than the standard. In this way the comparative value of performances on the clock can be readily assessed even though races were run over different courses and over different distances.

Clearly from the above set of figures, the horse which won or finished close up second in the Goodwood race over five furlongs where the standard was bettered by 0.20 seconds would be an obvious first choice.

There is one problem with comparative times. Races are run on different going. Obviously it is much easier to run a fast time on firm or good ground than on soft or heavy. In assessing times, therefore, some experience is needed in making an appropriate allowance for ground conditions but the time test is so valuable in evaluating two-year-old form that the effort to acquire expertise in this area is well worth making.

One other factor should be considered when betting on two-year-olds. This is the time of year. The situation alters from month to month, so your approach needs to be fitted to changing circumstances very precisely. The following points should be borne in mind:

APRIL. The new season has hardly begun and most juveniles are unknown quantities. Try to find one good two-year-old bet each day and keep stakes to an absolute minimum.

MAY. Form has started to settle down but there are still plenty of youngsters which have yet to show their true potential and the going can be changeable. Stick to one bet a day but increase your stake slightly.

JUNE. By now a fairly clear picture of the new crop of two-year-olds has emerged and summer is officially here, so there should not be too many variations in going or form. Keep to a single selection but you can now bet with confidence.

JULY and AUGUST. Traditionally the best months of the year for the backer, July and August bring really fast ground and short-priced horses monopolise the winner's enclosure. Now is the time to cash in with two or even three selections a day, backed in singles, doubles and trebles with your maximum stake.

SEPTEMBER. Suddenly a lot of form becomes suspect. Many two-year-olds begin to show the effects of a long campaign, fields get more competitive and the going can change very quickly with variable weather conditions. Now you should drop stakes sharply and be careful not to dissipate gains from a successful spring and summer.

OCTOBER. Every horse is competing for its winter training bill, fields are huge and heavy ground plays havoc with form. Long before November comes you should have closed your betting book for the year.

So a fully planned programme of two-year-old betting has been mapped out. The three basic rules will give you a small group of potential bets each day. The final process of selection gives you plenty of scope to exercise personal skill. The 'SPECIALIST' System is thus interesting to work. In the hands of a careful operator, the system has all the prerequisites of successful method of backing horses.

2
The 'PRESS SPECIALS' Form Plan gets the best from your racing page

Facts and figures are important to any serious follower of racing. For the system operator they are absolutely essential. Fortunately we have never had it so good in terms of the racing coverage offered regularly by the national press. Detailed race cards with extensive form analysis and skilfully compiled betting forecasts, course statistics plus selections by acknowledged experts are a feature of the sporting pages of every popular newspaper. Nowadays the racing fan is given so much help that winning might seem a relatively simple task.

Of course it isn't simple, far from it. Even with the embarrassment of riches to be found in the racing pages, the wheat still has to be sorted from the chaff. The problem of finding enough winners to yield a profit over a reasonable period of time defeats most of us.

One possible answer is to look very closely at the tips given by the racing correspondents retained by the various newspapers. These men are professionals; they travel regularly to race meetings and they are paid to make a thorough study of every aspect of form. A method of betting based on their selections ought to offer a reasonably trouble-free road to success.

In fact the typical newspaper correspondent who makes a selection in every race manages an overall ratio of approximately one winner to three losers. At first sight this may not seem too satisfactory. It is a worse average, for instance, than the general percentage of winning favourites. It must be remembered, however, that the newspaper man's successes include a spread of winners at all prices up to the occasional 20–1 outsider. The fact that the striking rate of winning press selections does not depend on strings of horses at short prices prompts me to suggest that in terms of potential profit they are probably the best of all readily available betting propositions.

Some backers have a favourite tipster whose selections they follow regularly. Almost everyone has a clear preference for one correspondent above all others, even if they don't always take his advice as a standard betting procedure. The 'PRESS SPECIALS' System recommends that you do concentrate on the tips of your preferred newspaper man. The idea, however, is not to back his choice in every race but to single out only those runners which have the highest statistical chance of winning.

One way of doing this is to examine closely the performance figures of each horse he names. Performance figures are of course the record of a horse's placings on its last three outings which precedes the name of each runner on the standard race card. It is a well known fact that some three-figure combinations produce a far greater overall percentage of winners than others. Moreover the best of them show a remarkably high level of consistent success. My figures based on a full year of racing, Flat and jumps, are as follows:

131	33%
121	32%
111	30%
311	29%
221	29%
211	28%

231	28%
321	28%
122	28%
421	27%

The operating instructions for the 'PRESS SPECIALS' Plan are very simple and require only a few minutes' work each day. Examine every selection of your chosen tipster and pick out only those which have recorded one of the above performance combinations over their last three outings. In this way you locate up to two or three horses per day that have a double plus factor in their favour. They must be regarded as bets of the highest quality.

Nothing guarantees a profit in racing but this system has real potential for consistent success. In summer or winter you are automatically on some of the best bets your newspaper has to offer. Moreover the selective process need not end there. The discerning backer who uses his own judgement to pick and choose may be able to pinpoint one horse a day which comes close to being the perfect wager.

3

The 'BEST OUTSIDER' Formula for long-priced coups on the Flat

Backing favourites or near-favourites is not to everyone's taste. Prices in the nature of things will be on the short side, so to make anything at the game you need a consistently high percentage of winners. Outsiders on the other hand allow for a much wider margin of error. A regular policy of backing horses at the long end of the market will almost certainly result in fewer winners but over a period of time big odds may well compensate for this. Many backers, I feel, would welcome a system for outsiders provided it offers a real prospect of a decent gain on a reasonably prolonged series of selections.

The 'BEST OUTSIDER' Formula is such a system. Clearly handicaps are the races in which a plan based on outsiders is most likely to succeed. They are more open than other kinds of races and winners and placed horses frequently start at good odds. The difficulty of course is to locate viable bets at long prices when the basis of any good system must be form. Well it is my belief that a combination of factors — one statistical and one form-related — can in fact be used to pick out an outsider with a real chance each day.

As far as statistics are concerned, a survey over a three-year period demonstrated beyond all doubt that in Flat handicaps horses near the top of the weights hold the best chance of success. Class tells in racing, so they say, and this is borne out by results in handicaps just as much as in other types of event.

Here are the figures which underline the point:

> 48% of the winners of all Flat handicaps are one of the top four in the weights.
> 62% of the winners come from the first six in the weights.

These percentages point to trends in the overall pattern of results that are just too pronounced to ignore. Whilst winners can and do come from lower down in the handicap, statistically they are most likely to stem from the group which heads the weights.

As for form without which no system can hope to succeed, even one based on outsiders, it is a fact that many horses with sound win and placed form in recent runs do perform well, even though the market gives them only a slender chance of success. For example any horse good enough to reach the first four in each of its last three races must have some kind of chance of reaching a place again and may even win. This is true whatever the odds fixed by the betting ring.

The fundamental idea behind the 'BEST OUTSIDER' Formula is to combine these high-weight and form factors in order to pick out a horse at long odds that at the very least has a definite chance of running into a place.

In the first instance it is necessary to analyse each handicap on the day's cards from the point of view of weight. This is done by applying a sliding scale based on the number of runners in a race. It is logical that in a really big field we should examine a wider range of high-weighted horses than in a race with fewer runners. Handicaps of ten or less contestants are ignored because starting prices are unlikely to be long enough for system purposes. The scale is as follows:

HANDICAPS

of 15 or more runners: consider the first six in the weights

of 14 to 13 runners: consider the first five in the weights

of 12 to 11 runners: consider the first four in the weights

Using this scale for every handicap on a given day, list any horse which ran first, second, third or fourth in each of its last three public outings and which figures in the specified weight range for the number of runners in the field. So on a typical day's racing we might get six possibilities:

HANDICAPS

Runners	Position in Weights	Form Figures	Betting Forecast Price
17	5th	234	10–1
16	6th	321	3–1
15	2nd	241	12–1
13	2nd	213	6–1
12	4th	332	7–1
11	3rd	114	5–2

The system rule is to take the horse at the best forecast price from all the possible qualifiers. In the above example the day's best outsider would therefore be the third on the list, that is the one priced at 12–1. It is in the right weight group in relation to the size of its field, it has the necessary form figures and is best-priced of all the potential bets. Since the odds are good and the horse is consistent enough to usually reach a place, each-way betting is both justified and desirable.

Does the system work? Well, here is a typical set of results for a month's racing, the month in which I happen to be writing:

18

WEEK 1: 2nd 9–1, W 9–1, 2nd 9–1, UNP,
2nd 14–1, UNP.
WEEK 2: UNP, W 3–1, UNP, UNP, UNP, 4th
10–1 (place betting).
WEEK 3: 3rd 11–1, W 9–2, UNP, 2nd 11–2,
UNP, 3rd 14–1.
WEEK 4: UNP, UNP, W 17–2, UNP, UNP,
UNP.

At a stake of 1 point each-way on all bets this works out at a pre-tax profit of 11½ points. The place bets have been calculated at 1/5 the win odds, even though most bookmakers offer better rates in handicaps with very big fields. Since these concessions can vary from layer to layer, for the sake of uniformity the standard rate has been used. The overall picture is accurate enough, even though the actual profit may be slightly greater.

Now a gain of 11½ points on a 24-bet sequence may not seem spectacular but given the consistency with which the system turned up long-priced winners and placers, it would be fair to assume that this might grow into a goodish sum over a lengthy period of betting. Either as a singles bet or as a profit-booster in multiple wagers involving doubles, trebles and accumulators, the 'BEST OUTSIDER' is a horse to be reckoned with every racing day.

4
The 'MIDSUMMER' Method for doubles, trebles and accumulators in selected non-handicaps

July and August are the backer's months. Form on the Flat has had plenty of time to settle down and firm ground sees small fields and more predictable results than at any other time of the year. Favourites and near-favourites go in with monotonous regularity. The 'MIDSUMMER' Method offers a sporting chance of cashing in when circumstances are most favourable to the punter.

The general percentage of winning favourites rises sharply in every kind of race during the summer months but there are a number of categories which according to the records are particularly good for backers. These include maiden races for two-year-olds and non-handicaps confined to three-year-olds, of which stakes races, sellers and maidens are the three main types.

As far as two-year-old maiden races are concerned, the fact that they are restricted to non-winners means that competition is not strong. One or two horses usually stand out on what they have achieved so far and for the most part they are able to confirm their form advantage in the actual race. In this they are helped by midsummer conditions, for with the exception of known mudlarks, the average thoroughbred is more reliable on fast ground than any other type of going.

Much the same reasons account for the high success rate of winning favourites in three-year-old non-handicaps. Halfway through the season on firm surfaces, the form of well-exposed three-year-olds works out exceptionally well. In maiden races opposition is not strong and the fancied horses have it to themselves. Clever trainers can exploit a consistent three-year-old in sellers. As for stakes races, many of these feature class horses which almost by definition can be expected to run to form. So three-year-olds competing on equal terms without the intervention of the handicapper offer relatively easy pickings for the discerning backer of favourites.

The system bet, therefore, is to back the market leaders in the above types of races. As you would expect, a very high percentage of winners may be counted upon. My statistics show a small level stake profit in most years. The problem is the poor odds returned about some, but by no means all of the winners. The obvious solution is to back them in doubles and trebles which can be an effective way of boosting profits from short-priced selections.

If you get hold of an old form book and check the method, you will find that it is not beyond the bounds of possibility that four or five system bets may win on the same day. There is plenty of racing at this time of year, usually three meetings a day even in the middle of the week, so there are many opportunities to land successful cumulative wagers. By including accumulators whenever possible, there is every prospect of some really good payouts. You only need to land an all-correct bet on a handful of occasions during the two-month period to be assured of a sound overall profit.

In fact bookmakers are very wary of this type of betting but multiple win bets on unnamed favourites are acceptable in betting shops. Providing you indicate that you want the unnamed starting price favourite and clearly show the time and meeting of the races involved, specifying the appropriate number of doubles, trebles and accumulators with the correct stakes, you should have no trouble in getting your bet on. You will not be your bookmaker's ideal customer, for you are definitely taking advantage of favourable conditions in favoured races. However any pangs of conscience you may have about exploiting the poor old bookie will soon disappear if you are lucky enough to land a few really big bets.

5

The 'STAR CHOICE' Method selects only the very best bets for the Flat's top weight-for-age races

Many readers will be familiar with the Jockey Club's 'Pattern Race' classification by which the top non-handicaps for the various age groups are divided into Group 1, Group 2, Group 3 races according to their status and value. The 'STAR CHOICE' Method concentrates only on the very highest echelon of Flat racing, that is the Group 1 weight-for-age races run over middle distances. Chief amongst these are the five Classic races — Newmarket's 2000 and 1000 Guineas, the Derby and Oaks at Epsom and finally the St. Leger run at Doncaster in the autumn. Other races which fall into the elite category are four big events in July and August. They are the Eclipse Stakes (Sandown), the King George VI and Queen Elizabeth Stakes (Ascot), the Sussex Stakes (Goodwood) and the sponsored Gold Cup (York). The Champion Stakes decided at Newmarket near the end of the season completes the cycle of the greatest races in the British Calendar.

The 'STAR CHOICE' approach is ultra selective and seeks to pinpoint only the best for the best. To win any one of this sequence of top races takes a horse of the highest class. Hence the basic premise of the system:

> *In such races any horse which has failed to win its last two races in similar or lesser company cannot be said to have a good chance.*

Think about this carefully. Spelled out like that the

idea seems self-evident but examine any of the top weight-for-age races and see how many runners you can eliminate with it. In the majority of cases most of the candidates fail to measure up to the standard. Yet if a horse has failed recently in inferior or even similar company, how can you be confident about it winning one of the great races which bring together the best horses from the leading stables in England, Ireland and sometimes France? If, on the other hand, we confine ourselves only to those animals which have achieved the comparatively rare feat of two recent victories in roughly the same standard of racing, then surely we have something to bet on.

The 'STAR CHOICE' Method has therefore only one simple rule:

> *In the races named above as being the top weight-for-age races on the Flat back any horse which has won both its two most recent outings, provided at least one of them was a Group 1, 2 or 3 event.*

Group categories for big races are shown clearly in form books and in the form summaries that appear in the racing papers on the day of the race, so there should be no difficulty about determining qualifiers.

The formula will often single out only one horse for a big race. Sometimes two or three will qualify. You are strongly advised to back them all. Unlike most of the runners, these horses boast unbeaten form in approximately similar company. Given the prestige at stake they are sure to be trying for their lives. They are bound to go close to winning. If you have to back more than one in the same race, the extra stakes are justified to make certain of being on the right one.

What about starting prices? 'All odds on,' I can hear the cynics saying. Not true, for opinions always take a wide range in the great races and the prices for qualifiers can extend to 10–1 and occasionally even more. Of course there will be short-priced favourites too but whilst there is no such thing as a racing certainty, records show that they are in the banker class.

The 'STAR CHOICE' System isolates only the cream of the bets in the top sphere of international racing. Look for yourself in racing annuals for past years and check the idea out. You will be agreeably surprised not only by the number of winners but also by the odds sometimes freely available about them. It must be remembered that the performance of any racehorse, even one of the very highest class, is to some extent governed by the laws of chance but these animals definitely have unrivalled potential as betting propositions.

6
The 'KEY RACES' Method for big race winners

Most of the big races in the British Calendar have
been established for well over a century and a half.
Moreover the actual fixture list has changed little in
terms of the time of year at which the most
important events are run. In these circumstances it is
not surprising that definite patterns should have
evolved which determine how horses are readied for
big races. Individual trainers may have their own
methods of preparing horses on the gallops but
season after season the big winners follow similar
paths to success. These are governed by the far from
limitless opportunities offered by a largely
unchanging programme of meetings and races. This
is the justification for the 'key race' theory of
betting. In many cases the key to the results of top
races is to be found in earlier races which
traditionally provide important clues. It is simply a
question of discovering the seasonal pattern and
applying it to the current year.

Below is an analysis of the top races according to
the key race idea. Allied to the study of form, it
should enable you to back a lot of big winners.

THE CLASSICS

Readers are referred to the 'STAR CHOICE' Method
earlier in the book but the following is a more specific
guide which may help you to choose between several
possible candidates.

1000 Guineas (1m., Newmarket, early May)
The first Classic for three-year-old fillies comes
barely a month after the start of the new Flat season.

There are a number of trials in April which can often confuse the picture. The best of them in recent years has been the Nell Gwyn Stakes at Newmarket. On the other hand there are plenty of examples in the record book of a filly succeeding first time out in the big race. Two-year-old form, therefore, is very much the key. One of the leading six fillies in the Free Handicap for Two-Year-Olds based on the previous season's racing, plus the top-rated Irish and French filly if they contest the race, form a group which usually includes the winner.

2000 Guineas (1m., Newmarket, early May)
As in the 1000, two-year-old form is the best guide to the first Classic for colts (although fillies are eligible to run). One of the leading ten horses in the Two-Year-Old Free Handicap quite frequently lands the prize. The Middle Park and the Dewhurst Stakes at Newmarket and the Gimcrack Stakes at York are big juvenile races which often throw up live contenders that sometimes win. Again early season trials can be misleading and the 2000 Guineas is very much a race to treat with caution in betting terms.

Derby Stakes (1½m., Epsom, early June)
The Derby is an international event featuring challengers from England, Ireland and France. There are many trials but no one race consistently provides the best clue. The race is seldom won by anything but a genuine stayer. Hence the failure in the race of so many 2000 Guineas winners whose speed is often blunted by the extra four furlongs. Favourites or near-favourites dominate the race, so look for a well-backed candidate which has won at or close to a mile and a half in top company. This usually cuts the field down to a few live contenders from which the winner may come. An interesting feature in recent times has been the number of winners which were given an easy time at two. Top-class two-year-old

27

form is, therefore, no longer a necessary credential, as was the case even ten years ago.

Oaks Stakes (1½m., Epsom, early June)
Winners of the 1000 Guineas have an outstanding record and placed horses from the first Classic also do well. Otherwise the race mostly falls to a filly which has won well over a mile and a half and is preferably unbeaten at three.

St Leger Stakes (1¾m., Doncaster, early September)
The first two in the Epsom Derby, the winner of the Irish Derby and the winner of the Great Voltigeur Stakes at York in August will provide a group that has accounted for a great many winners over the years. On the other hand the distance of the St Leger is almost a marathon by modern breeding standards and outsiders do better than in any other Classic.

WEIGHT-FOR-AGE AND CONDITION RACES

Ormonde Stakes (Im. 5f., Chester, early May)
This important early season test for senior horses seldom falls to anything but a form horse. If one of the first three in either the previous season's Derby or St Leger contests the race, then you have something of a banker bet.

Coronation Cup (1½m., Epsom, early June)
Epsom's big middle-distance event used to be farmed by Classic winners of the previous year but nowadays with so many good horses retiring to stud at the end of their three-year-old season, the race usually goes to one of the second eleven. The Jockey Club Stakes at the Guineas meeting, the Aston Park Stakes at Newbury and Goodwood's Clive Graham Stakes, both in May, have proved useful key races in recent years.

St James's Palace Stakes (1m., Ascot, mid-June)
One of Royal Ascot's showpieces, the race is open to
three-year-olds only. It tends to be monopolised by
placed horses in the 2000 Guineas. Also the winner
of the Irish 2000 should be carefully considered if a
runner.

Coronation Stakes (1m., Ascot, mid-June)
Fillies which ran first or second in the 1000 Guineas
at Newmarket are ready-made choices most seasons.
Apart from the occasional shock result, they have a
remarkably high scoring rate.

Lancashire Oaks (1½m., Haydock, early July)
This important race for staying three-year-old fillies
is a recognised consolation prize for Oaks failures.
Any filly which finished in the first half dozen at
Epsom should go close.

Eclipse Stakes (1¼m., Sandown, early July)
The Eclipse Stakes is a race of the very highest class
open to three-year-olds and upwards over the
specialist distance of ten furlongs. It takes a real
top-notcher to win, so concentrate on horses which
are unbeaten in the current season. The Prince of
Wales's Stakes at Royal Ascot has been the best
single guide in recent years.

King George VI and Queen Elizabeth Stakes
(1½m., Ascot, late July)
The winners of the Epsom and Irish Derbies and the
Eclipse Stakes invariably do well in this big
international event. Fillies and mares have an
excellent record and should always be noted if they
have top-class form.

Sussex Stakes (1m., Goodwood, late July)
Three-year-olds dominate this showdown between
the best milers at Glorious Goodwood. The most

accurate guide tends to be the St James's Palace Stakes, whilst the 2000 and 1000 Guineas have an obvious bearing. However it may not always be easy to pick the right one.

Gold Cup (1¼m., York, mid-August)
One of the very few recent additions to the top echelon of racing, York's big sponsored test takes a great deal of winning. Since its inception the first three in the Epsom Derby have provided the biggest proportion of winners.

Yorkshire Oaks (1½m., York, mid-August)
The form of the top staying fillies has moved on a bit since the beginning of June, so whilst the Epsom Oaks does still sometimes give a clue, later races such as the Ribblesdale Stakes at Royal Ascot, the Nassau Stakes at Goodwood and in particular the Irish Oaks at the Curragh are more likely to provide the answer.

Park Hill Stakes (1¾m., Doncaster, early September)
The extra distance of the fillies' St Leger can produce shocks and the race is often won by an improving sort hitherto regarded as only a handicapper. The Galtres Stakes at York's big August meeting sometimes throws up a live contender. Best form among the established Classic fillies is usually represented by the Yorkshire and Irish Oaks.

Champion Stakes (1¼m., Newmarket, mid-October)
Run over the straight ten furlongs at Newmarket in the autumn when even some of the best horses have had enough for the season, this prestige weight-for-age race is one of the trickiest in the Calendar. An English Classic winner, either a three-year-old or a four-year-old, and not necessarily the one at the shortest price, is often the best

solution. Fillies are at their peak at this time of year and they have an outstanding record in recent runnings.

THE CUP RACES

Gold Cup (2½m., Ascot, mid-June)
In an age of speed very few horses are able to produce top-class acceleration at the end of a marathon distance. Potential winners are therefore seldom difficult to spot and outsiders have a poor record. The most reliable trial in recent times has been the Henry II Stakes over two miles at the Sandown May meeting. The Prix du Cadran, the French equivalent, sometimes throws up a challenger or two but French stayers no longer enjoy the predominance they once did, so the face value of the form can be deceptive.

Goodwood Cup (2m. 5f., Goodwood, late July)
An obvious choice is the Gold Cup winner if that horse contests the race but the price is bound to be short and the Goodwood stamina test has yielded its share of shocks over the years. A good trial in the last decade or so has been a handicap, the Northumberland Plate at Newcastle. Any horse which runs prominently in the Plate has a sporting chance in a race that these days rarely attracts a competitive field.

Doncaster Cup (2¼m., Doncaster, early September)
The principals in the Gold Cup have had plenty of time to recover from their exertions and the big Ascot race is the best key to this event. The Queen's Vase and the Queen Alexandra Stakes are two other stamina tests at the Royal meeting which sometimes provide a clue. The Goodwood Cup is another relevant race.

Jockey Club Cup (2m., Newmarket, early October)

Horses which ran well in the Goodwood and Doncaster Cups are ready-made candidates amongst the established stars but this race sometimes goes to an up-and-coming stayer which has shown good recent form as evidence of the improvement that can come with maturity.

TOP SPRINTS

King's Stand Stakes (5f., Ascot, mid-June)
Although open to older horses, this big sprint has been monopolised by three-year-olds in recent seasons. Look out for an improving horse of that age which has shown up well in sprint non-handicaps earlier in the season. The most instructive key race is the Temple Stakes over the minimum trip of Sandown in late May. Also the Duke of York Stakes at York earlier in the month can provide a useful clue.

July Cup (6f., Newmarket, early July)
Keys to the July Cup are the King's Stand Stakes and the Cork and Orrery Stakes at Royal Ascot. If either or both of the winners of these two races run but are opposed in the market, then you should be quick to take the hint, for the July Cup usually goes to the favourite or a near-favourite.

William Hill Sprint Championship (5f., York, mid-August)
Formerly known as the Nunthorpe Stakes, this five-furlong dash is generally regarded as the most important sprint in the Calendar. Whatever contradictions are to be found in recent form, the winners of the King's Stand Stakes and the July Cup have a habit of confirming their superiority in a race that usually decides the sprint crown for the season.

Diadem Stakes (6f., Ascot, late September)
Most of the top sprinters clash in what is always a

hotly contested race. Recent form is more often than not the best guide towards the end of a long season and what happened in the Vernons Sprint Cup at Haydock at the beginning of the month is the most relevant guide.

BIG HANDICAPS

Lincoln Handicap (1m., Doncaster, late March)
Much depends on the draw in the season's first big handicap, so small stakes are advised. Fitness is the key with most runners making their seasonal debut. Look for those horses which have shown they come to hand early by winning in the first month of the previous season. Live candidates should also have good win and placed form in fair handicap company at the backend to have a real chance of success in this highly competitive race.

Chester Cup (2¼m., Chester, early May)
Run round Chester's tight turns, the race is not so much a test of bottomless stamina as it might first appear. Just as important is a top-class jockey who can judge the pace on the tricky track. Horses which have already recorded a win in the first weeks of the season should be noted. For a big handicap, most winners are surprisingly well fancied.

Royal Hunt Cup (1m., Ascot, mid-June)
There are numerous good mile handicaps in the weeks leading up to Ascot's annual cavalry charge, so there are no obvious key races that can be singled out. Not a race for outright favourites but the winner nearly always comes from the first half dozen in the betting. Big stables tend to monopolise the race and the small trainer is seldom able to make an impact.

Wokingham Handicap (6f., Ascot, mid-June)
One of the most open handicaps of the year, this big sprint is another race where heavy betting is asking

for trouble. In recent years the Bretby Handicap at the Newmarket Guineas meeting has established itself as a useful trial.

Northumberland Plate (2m., Newcastle, late June)
The Pitman's Derby, as the race is known, usually falls to a well-backed candidate. The Queen's Prize at Kempton in mid-April, the Chester Cup and the Ascot Handicap at the Royal meeting are three races for stayers that can give useful hints.

Stewards' Cup (6f., Goodwood, late July)
There is no key formula to the race with winners coming from many directions. However two factors are most important. Three-year-olds are just coming into their own against older horses at this time of year and this age group dominates the list of past winners. Also a high number in the draw is a virtual necessity for success.

Ebor Handicap (1¾m., York, mid-August)
There are no easy solutions to this most open of staying handicaps. The class of the race is always very high, so lightweights are up against it, save for the unexposed three-year-old which might just fool the handicapper. Valuable staying handicaps at Newmarket, Ascot and Goodwood are the best guides.

Ayr Gold Cup (6f., Ayr, late September)
An each-way bet on horses in the first three in the Portland Handicap at Doncaster's big September meeting often pays a dividend in the Ayr race. Also the winner of the Northumberland Sprint Trophy at Newcastle in August should be noted if a runner.

Cambridgeshire (1m. 1f., Newmarket, early October)
This is without doubt the most difficult handicap of the year. Horses which finished in the first four in

the Royal Hunt Cup represent good value and
sometimes win. In addition watch out for good-class
fillies with winning form. Autumn is their time of
year.

Cesarewitch (2¼m., Newmarket, mid-October)
Great reserves of stamina are needed for this
end-of-season marathon. Many winners are either
established stayers with a biggish weight to match
their form or improving three-year-olds
down at the bottom of the handicap. Well-backed
horses do particularly well.

The key race theory is not just hindsight. If you try
it out, you will be amazed how often history repeats
itself. There will of course be some failures but the
statistical record is there for those who wish to use it
to their advantage.

7

The 'BLUE PRINT' Method is specially designed to locate the outstanding jumping favourites of the day

When winter comes most punters turn to favourites as the likeliest source of a regular flow of winners. This is perfectly understandable. Despite the fact that National Hunt racing has become increasingly competitive in the last couple of decades, jumping favourites retain a remarkably high level of consistency. Elsewhere in this volume you will find a staking formula which aims to capitalise on successful runs of winning selections at short prices but you still have to pick the right favourites.

The problem has exercised some of the most ingenious minds in racing over the years and a number of suggestions have been put forward for providing automatic selections. Below I show an analysis of some of the most sensible of these. In each case a five-year cycle of National Hunt racing has been used as a yardstick.

	WINNING PERCENTAGE	AVERAGE ANNUAL PROFIT (+) or LOSS (−)
Longest distance chase of the day (including handicaps)	41.4%	+5 pts
Most valuable chase of the day (including handicaps)	42.7%	+4 pts

First non-handicap on the card (principal meeting)	39.2%	−16 pts
Last race on the card (principal meeting)	38.1%	−13 pts
Favourite quoted at the second shortest price in the betting forecast of all favourites (all meetings)	43.6%	+7 pts

It can be seen that some of these methods are fundamentally sound. Yet a seasonal profit which fails to reach double figures seems a poor reward for a period of betting that runs from November to March. On the other hand the general winning percentages are very encouraging. Clearly discrimination will pay and I list below a series of guidelines designed to separate the good bets from the bad. First however I show a set of statistics which complete the picture about jumping favourites backed overall with no attempt at selectivity.

	WINNING PERCENTAGE	AVERAGE ANNUAL PROFIT (+) or LOSS (−)
All non-handicap chases	37.3%	−24 pts
All non-handicap hurdles	43.7%	−5 pts
Novice chases (non-handicaps)	38.7%	−19 pts
Novice hurdles (non-handicaps)	44.1%	−4 pts
Best race on the card (4th)	42.4%	+3 pts
Worst race on the card (3rd)	34.1%	−28 pts

The two sets of figures given in this section should serve as the basis of your calculations but obviously it is necessary to pick and choose. In fact there are a number of factors whose worth cannot be easily demonstrated in statistical terms but which long experience has taught me must cut out many poor bets. Combined with the full analysis of jumping favourites set out above, they can only help to increase the ratio of winners to losers.

1) Back only favourites that were first or second last time out. There are plenty of false favourites even over the sticks. This simple rule ensures that you are at least backing animals with a basic form qualification which many market choices do not have.

2) Avoid betting at odds on. To my mind this is a golden rule which should be applied to all betting enterprises. With a failure rate of between 30 and 40%, odds on favourites are a bookmaker's benefit. I have yet to meet a bookie who isn't quite happy to lay even very large sums at odds on, for such wagers cannot hurt him but can quite often cripple a backer.

3) If you decide to back a favourite in a handicap, stick to small fields. I would make it an absolute rule not to bet in a race with more than ten runners. 'The bigger the field, the bigger the certainty' is perhaps the silliest of all racing maxims.

You now have before you a complete guide to backing favourites in winter, a 'BLUE PRINT' of all possibilities. The message behind everything that has been said is that it is absolutely vital to be selective. Personally I am impressed by the high percentage of winning favourites in novice hurdles. These races are seldom very competitive and if you can find a favourite at fair odds against that ran first or second last time out and which is trained by one of the dozen or so leading National Hunt trainers, then you definitely have something to bet on. But if on a given day there is no horse which fulfills these conditions, then you should be prepared to use the 'BLUE PRINT' to select an outstanding prospect in another category of race. Everything depends on what material is available at the time. Sometimes you will be unable to find even one favourite which can be backed with real confidence. In that case do not bet. In other words discriminate betting pays; betting for betting's sake most certainly does not.

Use the 'BLUE PRINT' wisely and well and you could achieve a percentage of winners that will surprise and delight you.

8

The 'OCCASIONAL' Jumping System pinpoints chasers and hurdlers at the peak of their form

Handicaps are framed with the express purpose of giving every horse in a race an equal chance. The system of additional penalties is designed to prevent an animal which makes a sudden dramatic improvement in form taking undue advantage in near-at-hand engagements before the weights can be reassessed according to the principle of equality. A detailed examination of the records will show that while penalties work well enough in Flat handicaps, they seem far less effective over the sticks.

Why this should be so is difficult to say. Perhaps the answer is that National Hunt racing is much more about jumping ability and stamina than it is about weight. Be that as it may, it is a fact that a good jumper once it nears its peak often goes from strength to strength. A penalty has very little stopping effect. The result is that despite extra burdens the horse goes on winning. The 'OCCASIONAL' System is designed to single out those penalised jumpers which represent the best bets in subsequent outings.

It could be that some readers are comparative newcomers to the sport and have yet to acquire a thorough knowledge of the finer points of the way penalties work in handicaps. Possibly some older hands at the game may not be fully conversant with this rather technical aspect of racing. I make no apologies, therefore, for going into the matter in some detail.

As everyone knows the weights for forthcoming handicaps are published well in advance in the Racing Calendar. Each race has a set of conditions attached to it whereby a horse which wins a race or races of a specified status after the closing date for entries is given an automatic penalty. This can be as little as three pounds for a minor success with steeper impositions for more than one win or a particularly important success. Here is an example:

THE JOHN BULL HANDICAP STEEPLE CHASE.
With £2,500 added to stakes for five yrs old and upwards. Penalties, after 7th March, a winner of a steeple chase 6lb. Of 2 steeple chases 10lb. Half penalties for horses originally handicapped at or above 11st 7lb.
THREE MILES AND ABOUT 100 YARDS.
(CLOSED 7th March).

These clauses are very much for the professional and in particular concern trainers who have to decide which races offer the best opportunities for their charges. Fortunately however all national newspapers, without quoting race conditions in full, do show in their daily race cards the fact that a horse is carrying a penalty. For example:

031 Blue Waters   A. Trainer 10–10–8 (5lb ex)

So Blue Waters has received a penalty of five pounds for its recent success. Horses so penalised are possible system qualifiers.

Backing all penalised horses would yield some winners but also a lot of losers. It is necessary to be selective. As I have already indicated, the form book shows that some jumpers which improve rapidly are capable of notching up a sequence of wins. These are the animals the 'OCCASIONAL' Method aims to locate.

Here is the basic system rule:

> *In handicap chases and hurdles back any horse which has won its last two outings and which is carrying a penalty in today's race.*

So we choose horses seeking a hat trick, a difficult but not infrequent feat for a jumper at the top of its form. The extra weight, far from being a warning sign, is in fact a positive recommendation. The horse has won twice but those who make the rules recognise the possibility that it may win again. Hence the penalty. The records suggest that where National Hunt handicappers are concerned, the possibility is a very real one, so much so that the additional weight is unlikely to stop the horse.

What about prices? Well system qualifiers run in handicaps, so there are very few really short-priced favourites. Most horses are at reasonable odds, from about 5–2 upwards, with one at as much as 10–1 every now and then. They will not all win but at these kinds of prices there is plenty of room for a good profit over a period of time given the luck which is essential in all racing ventures.

As its name implies, the 'OCCASIONAL' System does not throw up a large number of qualifiers. One or two bets a week and sometimes even less will not suit the betting temperament of everyone but the record shows that when you do find a system horse, quite often it is well worth waiting for.

9

The 'MULTI-LINK' Staking Formula maximises profits from short-priced selections

Although assured of plenty of winners, the confirmed favourite backer faces the constant problem of converting short-priced successes into a worthwhile profit. The 'MULTI-LINK' method of staking is one of the best systems ever devised for solving the difficulty.

Stakes are on single daily selections but the formula links up a series of doubles spread over several days in order to make the very best use of those winners that are backed. Moreover the maximum number of points at risk in any one week is known in advance. It is always fifteen.

The fifteen points which cover one bet a day for a full six-day week are divided up as follows:

$$5 \quad 4 \quad 3 \quad 2 \quad 1 \quad 0$$

These basic daily units increase according to winners backed but if the first five bets lose, then no double has materialised, so there would be no bet on Saturday.

On Monday the bet is always five points. After each winner combine the odds ($3 - 1 = 3 + 1 = 4$, $6 - 4 = 1½ + 1 = 2½$, $4 - 7 = 4/7 + 1 = 1\ 4/7$ and so on). Now add the resultant figure to each of the basic units for the remaining days including Saturday.

As an example suppose the first bet wins at 3–1. Then the remaining bets for the week would each be increased by four points ($3 + 1$) to get:

$$\frac{4}{4}=8 \quad \frac{3}{4}=7 \quad \frac{2}{4}=6 \quad \frac{1}{4}=5 \quad \frac{0}{4}=4$$

The second and third bets lose but on Thursday there is a 2–1 winner. As a result the stakes for Friday and Saturday become:

$$\frac{5}{3}=8 \quad \frac{4}{3}=7$$

Friday's selection is a loser but on Saturday you back a winner at 6–4, so the stakes and results for the six-day cycle have been:

Stakes	: 5	8	7	6	8	7	
Results	: 3–1	L	L	2–1	L	6–4	
Gains	: 15			12		10½	= 37½ pts
Losses	:	8	7		8		= 23 pts
						Overall profit	= 14½ pts

Now if the fifteen points had been invested at level stakes of 2½ points for each of the six days, the profit on this sequence would have amounted to only 8¾ points.

In other words provided you can be reasonably confident of picking around 50% winning favourites each week, then the 'MULTI-LINK' Formula should increase gains when compared with level stakes betting on the same sequence.

However, as with practically everything connected with betting on horses, there are drawbacks. It is only fair to admit that the formula loses against level stakes if i) you back only one winner in a week — the principle of linked doubles to boost profits fails to operate ii) you back two or even three winners at very short odds, all odds on or close to it — level stakes do better by a slight margin. In all other cases the formula scores and often quite handsomely.

For example examine this sequence of bets. Prices are far from exceptional, yet there is a healthy plus in favour of the 'MULTI-LINK' Formula over level stakes betting:

	BASIC UNITS	
MONDAY	5	
TUESDAY	4	
WEDNESDAY	3	+ 3½ = £6.50
THURSDAY	2	+ 3½ + 2¾ = £8.25
FRIDAY	1	+ 3½ + 2¾ = £7.25
SATURDAY	0	+ 3½ + 2¾ + 1 8/13 = £7.86

	RESULT	PROFIT OR LOSS
MONDAY	L	– £ 5
TUESDAY	W 5–2	+ £10
WEDNESDAY	W 7–4	+ £11.37
THURSDAY	L	– £ 8.25
FRIDAY	W 8–13	– £ 4.46
SATURDAY	W 5–4	+ £ 9.82
	Profit	= £22.40
	Level Stakes Profit	= £10.28

The 'MULTI-LINK' Formula was originally conceived as a series of double events arising from a single daily selection from Monday to Saturday. However you may feel that on a particular day there is no worthwhile wager. This does not mean that you cannot use the system. Provided it is applied to six consecutive selections on different days, the mathematical symmetry of the formula is retained. If you prefer not to bet every day, you simply think in terms of six bets and not in terms of days of the week thus:

Bet 1	Bet 2	Bet 3	Bet 4	Bet 5	Bet 6
5	4	3	2	1	0

This might represent a series of wagers spread as follows:

Bet 1	Bet 2	Bet 3
Monday	Wednesday	Friday
5	4	3

Bet 4	Bet 5	Bet 6
Saturday	Tuesday	Thursday
2	1	0

Moreover if you do depart in this way from the strict Monday to Saturday rota, there is now no need to miss a good wager on the sixth day should the first five in the series prove unsuccessful. Suppose Bets 1 to 5 lose in the above example. In that event your selection for Thursday could become Bet 1 with a 5-point stake in a new series of six bets.

In the case of a mathematical formula of this kind a great deal depends on prices in relation to the number of winners and losers. But if you are the kind of backer who finds it relatively easy to pick out one good thing a day, then 'MULTI-LINK' is for you. You need to avoid strings of odds on chances for the formula to do its work but it will always increase profits compared with level stakes on a reasonable turnover of winners at reasonable prices.

10
The 'WEEKLY PROGRESSIVE' Racing Method for regulated betting from Monday to Saturday

In most staking plans the backer is required to increase his stakes on a series of losers. An eventual winner, it is hoped, will pay off losses to date and still yield a profit. Frequently however too long a losing run and a winner at too short a price combine to defeat the idea. The sequence reaches the point where the chance of recovering losses, still less of showing a gain, finally disappears. With the 'WEEKLY PROGRESSIVE' Method stakes gradually diminish whilst prices increase. In this way it overcomes the fundamental deficiencies of the usual type of staking formula.

The plan works like this. You pick one horse each day of the racing week. Your selections should be based on sound form principles but the deciding factor in arriving at a final choice is the probable starting price. On Monday and Tuesday you look for a 2–1 shot. For the next two days you aim to find winners around 4–1. Your bets for Friday and Saturday are chosen from horses priced at about 6–1. The price requirements for particular days apply irrespective of the number of winners and losers you back.

Stakes are regulated in the following way:

Monday	2–1	3 pts
Tuesday	2–1	3 pts
Wednesday	4–1	1½ pts
Thursday	4–1	1½ pts

| Friday | 6–1 | 1 pt |
| Saturday | 6–1 | 1 pt |

Now you might well ask: why not begin by trying to pick a winner at 6–1? The answer is quite simply that it is easier to find one at 2–1. Obviously it is desirable to win as early in the week as possible but suppose you fail. You are faced with the choice of increasing stakes or selecting a better-priced winner. The pitfalls inherent in rising stake progressions have already been outlined. It must be far safer in the long term to try for winners at better prices. Now if things can be so arranged mathematically that you can actually reduce stakes without sacrificing the chance of a profit, then so much the better. This is exactly what the 'WEEKLY PROGRESSIVE' Method does.

If you begin by choosing a 6–1 selection, you might as well try to find one every day. Rather this plan aims at finding easy winners first so that there is cash in hand for later bets on horses at longer odds. The mathematics of the formula are such that you are quite justified in reducing stakes as the week advances. Either you have won or lost earlier in the week. If you have won, you want more gains but not at the risk of dissipating existing profits. Because it reduces stakes on longer-priced selections the formula achieves this double objective. If on the other hand you have lost early on, at the very least you want later bets to limit losses. Again the plan does the trick — stakes are diminishing and yet a winner or winners at good prices could still pull the fat out of the fire.

Of course a mathematical arrangement of prices and stakes, however sound, cannot produce profits out of thin air. You still have to back winners. Given that you are able to find some winners, the mathematics of the plan enable you to calculate in advance what you stand to win or lose. With just one winner from six bets you will have a maximum loss on the week of 4 points and possibly less. If you find two winners, and this is a reasonable expectation for the average competent backer, there will be an overall gain of between 3 and 7 points, depending on which horses actually win. Three winners guarantee a profit of at least 10½ points and possibly a good deal more. Four or more winners must yield a handsome return.

There is one problem. You are dependent on a betting forecast for the purpose of determining your daily selections. Fluctuations inevitably arise from market operations on the racecourse, so betting forecast predictions seldom correspond exactly to actual returned starting prices. In fact this is not too serious a draw-back. You may just as well gain as lose from this and in the long run things should even themselves out. The basic soundness of the formula will do the rest.

Finally it is necessary to say a word about methods of selection. Since the largest stakes go on to the 2–1 chances, special care must be exercised in choosing them. Here you are looking for out-and-out form horses but at the same time you must avoid the apparent good things which will start at really short prices close to odds on. For the 4–1 selections concentrate on second favourites with sound form in small fields where the favourite is quoted at upwards of 2–1 and so is not greatly fancied. The best way of singling out a 6–1 shot worth backing is to make a list of all horses in the right price category. Examine each in the light of recent form; winning or good placed form in similar company as revealed by a comparison of race values will put you onto some live candidates.

So the 'PROGRESSIVE' Method offers backers plenty of scope for making their own judgements. It is rigid in terms of selections being governed by the likely starting price but it is possible that a lot of backers who frequently find themselves spoilt for choice on a busy day's racing may well benefit from this discipline.

A mathematical plan is not an automatic road to racing riches but faulty staking is probably the biggest single reason why most backers lose. If you have a reasonable aptitude for picking winners, the 'WEEKLY PROGRESSIVE' Method will enable you to get the best from your successes.

11
The '19 WAYS TO WIN' Doubles Formula for summer or winter

A lot of backers achieve consistent results without ever quite managing to turn them into overall profit. They follow racing closely, know the form book well and can pick out two or three sound wagers each day that are certain to go close at decent prices. Yet in the long run they lose — too many near misses, good seconds and thirds, eat into the gains from winners. It could well be that you fall into this category of punter. If so, then the '19 WAYS TO WIN' Formula is one that you should definitely consider.

The trick is to link up one horse from one race with two from another in singles and each-way doubles. Suppose you select Horse A as a banker for the first race and decide on Horse B and Horse C for the second leg. The full bet is written as follows:

Race 1	Race 2
1 pt. win A	½ pt. win B
	½ pt. win C
1 pt. each-way double	A and B
1 pt. each-way double	A and C

For a 6-point stake this series this series of bets offers no less than nineteen chances of a return. The possible combinations are set out in full below.

1. A wins and B wins.   C places
. . . . 2 win singles, 1 win double, 2 place doubles.

2. A wins and C wins.   B places
. . . . 2 win singles, 1 win double, 2 place doubles.

3. A wins and B wins.   C loses
. . . . 2 win singles, 1
win double, 1 place double.

4. A wins and C wins.   B loses
. . . . 2 win singles, 1
win double, 1 place double.

5. A wins and B places.   C places
. . . . 1 win single, 2 place
doubles.

6. A wins and B places.   C loses
. . . . 1 win single, 1 place
double.

7. A wins and C places.   B loses
. . . . 1 win single, 1 place
double.

8. A wins and B loses.   C loses
. . . . 1 win single.

9. B wins and A places.   C places
. . . . 1 win single, 2 place
doubles.

10. B wins and A places.   C loses
. . . . 1 win single, 1 place
double.

11. B wins and C places.   A loses
. . . . 1 win single.

12. B wins and A loses.   C loses
. . . . 1 win single.

13. C wins and A places.   B places
. . . . 1 win single, 2 place
doubles.

14. C wins and A places.   B loses
. . . . 1 win single, 1 place
double.
52

15. C wins and B places.   A loses
. . . . 1 win single.

16. C wins and A loses.   B loses
. . . . 1 win single.

17. A places and B places.   C places
. . . 2 place doubles.

18. A places and B places.   C loses
. . . 1 place double.

19. A places and C places.   B loses
. . . 1 place double.

Each-way doubles are definitely value bets for the careful punter. The '19 WAYS TO WIN' System with its clever combination of win singles and each-way doubles on three horses has tremendous scope. Many of the winning permutations will produce a really good gain on the day. Other patterns of results will recover some or all of your stake. You thus have plenty of insurance against those all-too-frequent near misses that usually mean total failure. You even have two chances of finding the winner in one race with very little wastage of stakes. Since place betting at fractions of the win odds is involved, a lot depends on prices. Clearly short-priced favourites should be avoided and whilst the banker should be an obvious form horse at fair odds, it is often worth taking a chance with a selection at a really good price as a danger to the first choice in the second leg. In the hands of a skilled punter who knows the form and can pick out value-for-money wagers in the right races, this staking formula is in a class of its own.

12

The 'WEEKENDER' aims for regular profits with the chance of a really big win

For the most part the Treble Chance mentality is absent amongst followers of horse racing. Few punters seriously expect to make a fortune, even a small one, from the sport. In fact the majority do not try. By and large they look for small regular gains from their betting whilst hoping for an occasional nice touch measured in tens not thousands of pounds to make the whole thing worthwhile.

Yet there is absolutely no reason why multiple cumulative wagers should not be used to aim for a jackpot payout. If these can be arranged so that the prospect of smaller wins on a regular basis is retained, then such a bet must represent a really attractive proposition. The 'WEEKENDER' goes a long way towards achieving this dual aim.

Saturday always sees a lot of racing up and down the country with plenty of opportunities to sort out an above average number of good bets. The 'WEEKENDER' requires you to select six possible winners. Since the system is made up of doubles, trebles and accumulators, you do not need a series of rank outsiders to produce the big win that is its ultimate goal. A judicious mixture of well-backed form horses with one or two at longer prices will do very nicely. This should not be too much of a problem. There are lots of ways of finding winners at all kinds of odds outlined in the this volume.

Having chosen six horses in different races, number them 1 to 6 as in the example below. The system depends on a set of firm guarantees, so this order, once decided upon, must be adhered to throughout when writing the full bet.

1 Chesterfield
2 No Tricks
3 Gala Day
4 Extra Strain
5 Marcus Superbus
6 Directory

The sequence of doubles, trebles and accumulators which make up the 'WEEKENDER' is as follows:

DOUBLES
1 & 3   1 & 6   2 & 4   2 & 5   3 & 6   4 & 5
TREBLES
1, 2, & 5   1, 3 & 5   1, 4 & 6   2, 3 & 4
2, 3 & 6   4, 5 & 6
ACCUMULATORS
1, 2, 3 & 4   1, 2, 5 & 6   3, 4, 5 & 6
1, 2, 3, 4, 5 & 6

So in our example the whole bet would be:

Doubles	**Trebles**	**Accumulators**
Chesterfield	Chesterfield	Chesterfield
Gala Day	No Tricks	No Tricks
————————	Marcus	Gala Day
Chesterrfield	Superbus	Extra Strain
Directory	————————	————————
————————	Chesterfield	Chesterfield
No Tricks	Gala Day	No Tricks
Extra Strain	Marcus	Marcus
————————	Superbus	Superbus
No Tricks	————————	Directory
Marcus	Chesterfield	————————
Superbus	Extra Strain	Gala Day
————————	Directory	Extra Strain
Gala Day	————————	Marcus
Directory	No Tricks	Superbus
	Gala Day	Directory
	Extra Strain	

Extra Strain	No Tricks	Chesterfield
Marcus	Gala Day	No Tricks
Superbus	Directory	Gala Day
		Extra Strain
	Extra Strain	Marcus
	Marcus	Superbus
	Superbus	Directory
	Directory	

Each group of wagers has a definite guarantee. Two winners may produce a winning double; three guarantee it. Similarly a treble is certain with four winners and a possibility with only three. Five successes mean you must land a four-horse accumulator, although only four can do the trick. Multiple winners, therefore, can add up to an impressive array of doubles, trebles and four-timers and of course if all the selections win, every one of the sixteen separate bets, including the six-timer, must score.

In other words the 'WEEKENDER' Method is a balanced wager which can be used for a weekly tilt at a gigantic payout without sacrificing the possibility of regular small-scale profits. For the small backer there is every prospect of plenty of bread and butter. There might be quite a wait for the honey but the chance of it is always there.

RACECOURSE GUIDE

A track-by-track guide to the most significant betting
trends at all courses in Britain.

ASCOT

Right-handed. 1¾m triangular course with stiff 2½f
run-in. Straight mile.

Flat

Effect of the draw	None, except that over sprint distances in very big fields, high numbers have an advantage when there is some give in the ground.
Winning favourites	1st favourite 34% 2nd favourite 27% 2-Y-Os 42%
Most significant form	(1st, 2nd, 3rd, 4th last time out) from Haydock and Sandown. At the Royal meeting, horses which were first or second last time out at Haydock, Sandown and Newbury have an outstanding record.

National Hunt

Winning favourites	1st favourite 42% 2nd favourite 21%
Most significant form	(1st, 2nd, 3rd, 4th last time out) from Cheltenham and Newbury.

AYR

Left-handed. 1m 5f oval course with 4f run-in.
Straight 6f.

Flat
Effect of the draw	None.
Winning favourites	1st favourite 38%
	2nd favourite 26%
	2-Y-Os 45%
Most significant form	(1st, 2nd, 3rd, 4th last time out) from York.

National Hunt
Winning favourites	1st favourite 38%
	2nd favourite 27%

BANGOR-ON-DEE

Left-handed. 1½m round course.

National Hunt
Winning favourites	1st favourite 46%
	2nd favourite 26%

BATH

Left-handed. 1½m oval course with sharp final bend
and 3½f straight.

Flat
Effect of the draw	Low-drawn horses running nearest the rails are naturally favoured on the turning course (races of seven furlongs and a mile). In sprints, the slight bend to the left on the run-in also favours low numbers.
Winning favourites	1st favourite 40%

	2nd favourite 21%
	2-Y-Os 44%
Most significant form	(1st, 2nd, 3rd, 4th last time out) from Salisbury.

BEVERLEY

Right-handed. 1m 3f oval course with uphill
2½f run-in.

Flat

Effect of the draw	High numbers have a big advantage over the 5-furlong course.
Winning favourites	1st favourite 34%
	2nd favourite 26%
	2-Y-Os 38%

BRIGHTON

Left-handed. 1½m horsehoe-shaped course. Run-in
3½f with stiff uphill finish.

Flat

Effect of the draw	Low numbers are generally held to be best in sprints, but a fast break is perhaps even more important.
Winning favourites	1st favourite 44%
	2nd favourite 24%
	2-Y-Os 49%
Most significant form	(1st, 2nd, 3rd, 4th last time out) from Brighton itself.

CARLISLE

Right-handed. 1m 5f undulating, oval course. 3½f
run-in. 6f course joins round track on a curve.

Flat

Effect of the draw

Traditionally high numbers are best on the round course and low numbers have the advantage in sprints. In practice a good horse can win from any draw.

Winning favourites

1st favourite 37%
2nd favourite 26%
2-Y-Os 42%

National Hunt

Winning favourites

1st favourite 39%
2nd favourite 30%

Most significant form

(1st, 2nd, 3rd, 4th last time out) from Carlisle itself.

CARTMEL

Left-handed. Flat 1m round course.

National Hunt

Winning favourites

1st favourite 34%
2nd favourite 24%

CATTERICK

Left-handed. 9f oval course with sharp downhill turn into 3f straight. 5f dog-leg.

Flat

Effect of the draw

Low numbers have some advantage in 5-, 6- and 7-furlong races but a quick break and the ability to handle the track are far more important on this sharp course where

	the big, long-striding horse can be seriously inconvenienced.
Winning favourites	1st favourite 39%
	2nd favourite 24%
	2-Y-Os 46%
Most significant form	(1st, 2nd, 3rd, 4th last time out) from Catterick itself.

National Hunt

Winning favourites	1st favourite 38%
	2nd favourite 22%

CHELTENHAM

Left-handed. Galloping 1½m oval course. Very stiff uphill finish.

National Hunt

Winning favourites	1st favourite 39%
	2nd favourite 24%
Most significant form	(1st, 2nd, 3rd, 4th last time out) from Newbury.

The first half a dozen or so home in the Mackeson Gold Cup in early November are well worth following in all their subsequent races for the rest of the season.

CHEPSTOW

Left-handed. 2m oval course with 5f run-in. Straight mile.

Flat

Effect of the draw	Low numbers are usually said to be best in all races, especially on soft going,

	but it would be a mistake to make too much of this.
Winning favourites	1st favourite 40%
	2nd favourite 28%
	2-Y-Os 45%

National Hunt

Winning favourites	1st favourite 38%
	2nd favourite 28%
Most significant form	(1st, 2nd, 3rd, 4th last time out) from Cheltenham.

CHESTER

Left-handed. Very tight, flat, circular course of just over a mile. 1f run-in.

Flat

Effect of the draw	In all sprints, low numbers have an advantage. Over the minimum distance this bias is very pronounced.
Winning favourites	1st favourite 37%
	2nd favourite 27%
	2-Y-Os 48%

DEVON AND EXETER

Right-handed. 2m undulating course.

National Hunt

Winning favourites	1st favourite 42%
	2nd favourite 26%
Most significant form	(1st, 2nd, 3rd, 4th last time out) from Newton Abbot.

DONCASTER

Left-handed. Flat, galloping, conical-shaped course of nearly 2m with 4½f run-in. Straight mile.

Flat

Effect of the draw	Low numbers used to be at a big disadvantage in large fields on the straight course (races up to a mile) but course alterations seem to have done a great deal to counteract this. Low numbers do best on soft ground.
Winning favourites	1st favourite 34% 2nd favourite 25% 2-Y-Os 46%
Most significant form	(1st, 2nd, 3rd, 4th last time out) from Newmarket.

National Hunt

Winning favourites	1st favourite 42% 2nd favourite 24%
Most significant form	(1st, 2nd, 3rd, 4th last time out) from Newcastle.

EDINBURGH

Right-handed. 1¼m oval course with 4f run-in. Straight 5f.

Flat

Effect of the draw	High numbers have a slight advantage over seven furlongs and a mile.
Winning favourites	1st favourite 37% 2nd favourite 24% 2-Y-Os 43%
Most significant form	(1st, 2nd, 3rd, 4th last time out) from Newcastle.

EPSOM

Left-handed. 1½m switchback course shaped like a horseshoe. Straight 5f is downhill for four furlongs with a sharp rise to the post.

Flat

Effect of the draw	Over sprint distances, a fast break and the ability to run downhill at speed are more important than the actual position at the start.
Winning favourites	1st favourite 39% 2nd favourite 25% 2-Y-Os 46%

FAKENHAM

Left-handed. 1½m undulating course with 250 yds run-in from final fence.

National Hunt

Winning favourites	1st favourite 47% 2nd favourite 31%

FOLKESTONE

Right-handed. 1m 3f undulating course. 3f run-in. Straight 6f.

Flat

Effect of the draw	Low numbers have a slight advantage in sprints.
Winning favourites	1st favourite 42% 2nd favourite 23% 2-Y-Os 50%

National Hunt

Winning favourites	1st favourite 42% 2nd favourite 29%

Most significant form	(1st, 2nd, 3rd, 4th last time out) from Folkestone itself.

FONTWELL

Left-handed. Hurdle course 1m round. Chase course figure of eight.

National Hunt

Winning favourites	1st favourite 43% 2nd favourite 26%
Most significant form	(1st, 2nd, 3rd, 4th last time out) from Newton Abbot.

GOODWOOD

Straight 6f. Right-handed loop for races from 7f to 1¾m joins straight course for 4f run-in. Distance races start reverse way up straight and turn left-handed into the loop.

Flat

Effect of the draw	High numbers have a big advantage in large fields in 6-furlong races. Over the minimum trip a quick start is more important than the draw.
Winning favourites	1st favourite 38% 2nd favourite 23% 2-Y-Os 47%
Most significant form	(1st, 2nd, 3rd, 4th last time out) from Newmarket. The first four in the Stewards' Cup at the big July meeting may show a profit if backed on all

their subsequent runs to
the end of the season.

HAMILTON

Right-handed. Straight 6f. Races from 1m 5f to 1m
40 yds start in reverse direction and are run round a
pear-shaped loop which rejoins the straight course
for a 4f run-in with a stiff uphill finish.

Flat

Effect of the draw	Low numbers are at a disadvantage in sprint races, particularly on soft ground.
Winning favourites	1st favourite 37%
	2nd favourite 26%
	2-Y-Os 47%

Form works out very badly at Hamilton. A
well-known trainer once remarked: 'If you want to
get a good horse beaten, take it to Hamilton.'

HAYDOCK

Left-handed. 1m 5f flat, oval course with 4f run-in.
Straight 6f.

Flat

Effect of the draw	A good horse can win from any draw.
Winning favourites	1st favourite 39%
	2nd favourite 24%
	2-Y-Os 51%

National Hunt

Winning favourites	1st favourite 33%
	2nd favourite 29%
Most significant form	(1st, 2nd, 3rd, 4th last time out) from Newcastle and Wetherby.

HEREFORD

Left-handed. 1½m course with 300 yds run-in from final fence.

National Hunt

Winning favourites	1st favourite 31%
	2nd favourite 29%
Most significant form	(1st, 2nd, 3rd, 4th last
	time out) from Worcester.

HEXHAM

Left-handed. 1½m round course. 250 yds run-in from final fence.

National Hunt

Winning favourites	1st favourite 42%
	2nd favourite 24%

HUNTINGDON

Right-handed. Flat, oval 1½m course.

National Hunt

Winning favourites	1st favourite 42%
	2nd favourite 23%

KELSO

Left-handed. 1m. 2f course.

National Hunt

Winning favourites	1st favourite 41%
	2nd favourite 27%

KEMPTON

Right-handed. 1m 5f triangular course with 3½f run-in. Straight 6f.

Flat

Effect of the draw	None.

| *Winning favourites* | 1st favourite 38%
2nd favourite 27%
2-Y-Os   44% |
| *Most significant form* | (1st, 2nd, 3rd, 4th last time out) from Newmarket. |

National Hunt
Winning favourites   1st favourite 42%
                          2nd favourite 28%

LEICESTER

Right-handed. 2m oval course with 5f run-in.
Straight mile.

Flat

| *Effect of the draw* | None. |
| *Winning favourites* | 1st favourite 42%
2nd favourite 23%
2-Y-Os   47% |

National Hunt
Winning favourites   1st favourite 42%
                          2nd favourite 29%

LINGFIELD

Left-handed. Easy 1m 3f round course with 4f
run-in. Straight 7f.

Flat

| *Effect of the draw* | High numbers have some advantage in races up to seven furlongs. Heavy going tends to nullify this advantage. |
| *Winning favourites* | 1st favourite 39%
2nd favourite 28%
2-Y-Os   48% |

Most significant form	(1st, 2nd, 3rd, 4th last time out) from Salisbury.

National Hunt
Winning favourites	1st favourite 43% 2nd favourite 24%

LIVERPOOL

Left-handed. Flat course is a 1m 3f oval with a 4f run-in. Straight 5f. Grand National course is 4m 856 yds.

Flat
Effect of the draw	Low numbers are best in races from six furlongs to a mile but on the straight 5-furlong course high numbers have the advantage.
Winning favourites	1st favourite 30% 2nd favourite 19% 2-Y-Os 31%

National Hunt
Winning favourites	1st favourite 26% 2nd favourite 21%

LUDLOW

Right-handed. 1½m oval course with 400 yds run-in from final fence.

National Hunt
Winning favourites	1st favourite 46% 2nd favourite 30%

MARKET RASEN

Right-handed. 1m 2f oval course.

National Hunt

Winning favourites	1st favourite 45%
	2nd favourite 23%
Most significant form	(1st, 2nd, 3rd, 4th last time out) from Market Rasen itself.

NEWBURY

Left-handed. 1m 7f galloping track with 4½f run-in. Straight mile.

Flat

Effect of the draw	None.
Winning favourites	1st favourite 35%
	2nd favourite 22%
	2-Y-Os 36%
Most significant form	(1st, 2nd, 3rd, 4th last time out) from Newmarket.

National Hunt

Winning favourites	1st favourite 39%
	2nd favourite 26%
Most significant form	(1st, 2nd, 3rd, 4th last time out) from Ascot.

NEWCASTLE

Left-handed. Oval 1¾m circuit with uphill 4f run-in. Straight 7f.

Flat

Effect of the draw	The round mile course definitely favours low numbers.
Winning favourites	1st favourite 41%
	2nd favourite 24%
	2-Y-Os 48%
Most significant form	(1st, 2nd, 3rd, 4th last time out) from Beverley.

National Hunt

Winning favourites	1st favourite 40%
	2nd favourite 31%
Most significant form	(1st, 2nd, 3rd, 4th last time out) from Ayr.

NEWMARKET

Rowley Mile Course. Right-handed. Dog-leg of 2m 2f with a straight stretch of 10f to an uphill finish. July Course. Right-handed. 2m dog-leg into a 1m straight, rising to the post.

Flat

Effect of the draw	None.
Winning favourites	1st favourite 31%
	2nd favourite 22%
	2-Y-Os 39%

Occasional raiders from the big Yorkshire stables are well worth noting.

NEWTON ABBOT

Left-handed. 1m oval course with 300 yds run-in from final fence.

National Hunt

Winning favourites	1st favourite 38%
	2nd favourite 28%
Most significant form	(1st, 2nd, 3rd, 4th last time out) from Devon and Exeter and Newton Abbot itself.

NOTTINGHAM

Left-handed. 1½m oval track with 4½f run-in. Straight 6f.

Flat

Effect of the draw	No advantage except high

numbers are favoured in sprints when the ground is soft.

Winning favourites 1st favourite 36%
2nd favourite 24%
2-Y-Os   36%

National Hunt
Winning favourites 1st favourite 37%
2nd favourite 26%

PERTH

Left-handed. 1½m circuit.

National Hunt
Winning favourites
1st favourite 44%
2nd favourite 26%

PLUMPTON

Left-handed. 1m 2f course with uphill finish.

National Hunt
Winning favourites 1st favourite 40%
2nd favourite 25%
Most significant form (1st, 2nd, 3rd, 4th last time out) from Plumpton itself.

PONTEFRACT

Left-handed. Pear-shaped course of 2m, almost all on the turn. 2f run-in with very stiff finish.

Flat
Effect of the draw Low numbers have some advantage in sprints.
Winning favourites 1st favourite 38%
2nd favourite 25%
2-Y-Os   46%

REDCAR

Left-handed. 2m oval course with 5f run-in. Straight
mile.

Flat

Effect of the draw	Over five and six furlongs, high numbers tend to dominate results.
Winning favourites	1st favourite 37% 2nd favourite 22% 2-Y-Os 43%
Most significant form	(1st, 2nd, 3rd, 4th last time out) from Thirsk.

RIPON

Right-handed. 1m 5f undulating, oval circuit with 5f
run-in. Straight 6f.

Flat

Effect of the draw	None.
Winning favourites	1st favourite 37% 2nd favourite 22% 2-Y-Os 39%

SALISBURY

Right-handed. Nearly straight 1m, uphill all the way.
Races of more than a mile on a loop, turning sharply
into the straight course for a 6½f run-in.

Flat

Effect of the draw	The advantage to high numbers on the straight mile course is nullified by placing the starting stalls in the centre of the track.
Winning favourites	1st favourite 36% 2nd favourite 23% 2-Y-Os 47%

Most significant form   (1st, 2nd, 3rd, 4th last
                                 time out) from Newbury.
Two-year-old winners at Salisbury often go on to
much better things at the top meetings.

SANDOWN

Right-handed. 1m 5f oval course with easy turns and
a stiff 4½f run-in. Separate 5f course also uphill.

Flat

Effect of the draw	In races up to a mile on the round course, high numbers are favoured. On the separate 5-furlong track there is a slight advantage to low numbers except if the going is soft when the reverse seems to apply.
Winning favourites	1st favourite 36% 2nd favourite 24% 2-Y-Os 41%
Most significant form	(1st, 2nd, 3rd, 4th last time out) from Sandown itself.

National Hunt

Winning favourites	1st favourite 39% 2nd favourite 25%
Most significant form	(1st, 2nd, 3rd, 4th last time out) from Ascot.

SEDGEFIELD

Left-handed. Sharp 1¼m course with downhill finish.

National Hunt

Winning favourites	1st favourite 43% 2nd favourite 27%

SOUTHWELL

Left-handed. Flat, round course of 10f.

National Hunt
Winning favourites   1st favourite 39%
                            2nd favourite 23%

STRATFORD

Right-handed. 1¼m flat, triangular course.

National Hunt
Winning favourites   1st favourite 38%
                            2nd favourite 21%

TAUNTON

Right-handed. Flat, oval track of 1¼m.

National Hunt
Winning favourites   1st favourite 39%
                            2nd favourite 24%

THIRSK

Left-handed. Flat, oval 1¼m course with 4f run-in. Straight 6f.

Flat
Effect of the draw   High numbers are definitely favoured in sprints.
Winning favourites   1st favourite 40%
                            2nd favourite 23%
                            2-Y-Os   49%

TOWCESTER

Right-handed. 1½m course with long climb over final 6f.

National Hunt

Winning favourites

1st favourite 45%
2nd favourite 24%

UTTOXETER

Left-handed. 1¼m oval, undulating course.

National Hunt

Winning favourites

1st favourite 43%
2nd favourite 26%

WARWICK

Left-handed. Circular 1¾m course with 2½f run-in. 5f dog-leg.

Flat

Effect of the draw

Low numbers have a definite edge in races up to seven furlongs. Soft going tends to offset this advantage.

Winning favourites

1st favourite 35%
2nd favourite 24%
2-Y-Os   43%

National Hunt

Winning favourites

1st favourite 37%
2nd favourite 25%

WETHERBY

Left-handed. 1½m course with long rise to finish.

National Hunt

Winning favourites

1st favourite 41%
2nd favourite 25%

Most significant form

(1st, 2nd, 3rd, 4th last time out) from Catterick.

WINCANTON

Right-handed. 1m 3f oval circuit. 200 yds run-in from final fence.

National Hunt
Winning favourites   1st favourite   40%
      2nd favourite 26%

WINDSOR

Right-handed. Flat 1½m figure of eight course. Straight 6f.

Flat
Effect of the draw	None.
Winning favourites	1st favourite 42%
	2nd favourite 24%
	2-Y-Os 49%
Most significant form	(1st, 2nd, 3rd, 4th last time out) from Windsor itself.

National Hunt
Winning favourites	1st favourite 41%
	2nd favourite 27%
	2-Y-Os
Most significant form	(1st, 2nd, 3rd, 4th last time out) from Newbury.

WOLVERHAMPTON

Left-handed. Pear-shaped course of 1m 5f, flat with easy turns. 5f run-in. 6f sprint course.

Flat
Effect of the draw	No advantage on the sprint track but on the turning 7-furlong and mile track low numbers are preferred.

Winning favourites	1st favourite 36%
	2nd favourite 22%
	2-Y-Os 44%
Most significant form	(1st, 2nd, 3rd, 4th last time out) from Wolverhampton itself.

National Hunt
| Winning favourites | 1st favourite 39% |
| | 2nd favourite 23% |

WORCESTER

Left-handed. Flat 1m 5f course with 4f run-in.

National Hunt
Winning favourites	1st favourite 38%
	2nd favourite 24%
Most significant form	(1st, 2nd, 3rd, 4th last time out) from Cheltenham.

YARMOUTH

Left-handed. 1m 5f oval course with 5f run-in. Straight mile.

Flat
Effect of the draw	High numbers do best over six furlongs.
Winning favourites	1st favourite 38%
	2nd favourite 24%
	2-Y-Os 43%

YORK

Left-handed. 2m horseshoe-shaped, galloping track with 5f run-in. Straight 6f and a 7f chute.

Flat
| Effect of the draw | None except that low numbers are definitely |

	favoured by soft ground in sprints.
Winning favourites	1st favourite 39% 2nd favourite 23% 2-Y-Os 44%
Most significant form	(1st, 2nd, 3rd, 4th last time out) from Newmarket.

The form from York, where the best horses from North and South meet, is very reliable and should always be highly respected when assessing future races.